LOCOMOTION PAPERS

THE DAVINGTON LIGHT RAILWAY

A World War I Narrow Gauge Railway in Kent

by
M. Minter Taylor

THE OAKWOOD PRESS

© Oakwood Press & M. Minter Taylor 2014

First edition published 1968
Reprinted 1986
Second Revised Edition published 2014

British Library Cataloguing in Publication Data
A Record for this book is available from the British Library
ISBN 978 0 85361 734 1
Typeset by Oakwood Graphics.
Repro by PKmediaworks, Cranborne, Dorset.
Printed by Gomer Press, Llandysul, Ceredigion.

All rights reserved. No part of this book may be reproduced or transmitted in any form or by any means, electronic or mechanical, including photocopying, recording or by any information storage and retrieval system, without permission from the Publisher in writing.

Cotton Powder Co. Manager Mr Arnold is greeted by gatekeeper C. Rivers *circa* 1915.
Fleur de Lis Heritage Centre

Rear cover: A Davington bound train emerges from Oare tunnel with marshland, and Whitstable, in the background. *Painting by the author*

Published by The Oakwood Press (Usk), P.O. Box 13, Usk, Mon., NP15 1YS.
E-mail: sales@oakwoodpress.co.uk
Website: www.oakwoodpress.co.uk

Contents

	Preface to Second Edition	5
	Introduction to First Edition	6
Chapter One	**Gunpowder: A Napoleonic Backlash**	7
	Davington and Faversham	7
	The Faversham explosives industry	8
	Davington	14
	Events leading up to the opening of the Davington Light Railway	15
Chapter Two	**The Railway**	17
	The route described	17
	Staff	21
	The timetable	25
	Fares and tickets	25
Chapter Three	**Rolling stock**	27
	Contractor's locomotives	27
	Main line locomotives	27
	Factory engines	29
	Carriages	35
	Wagons	37
Chapter Four	**Closure**	39
Chapter Five	**Lost and Found in Brazil**	43
Appendix One	**'Who Killed Cock Robin?'**	47
	Acknowledgements	48
	Bibliography	48

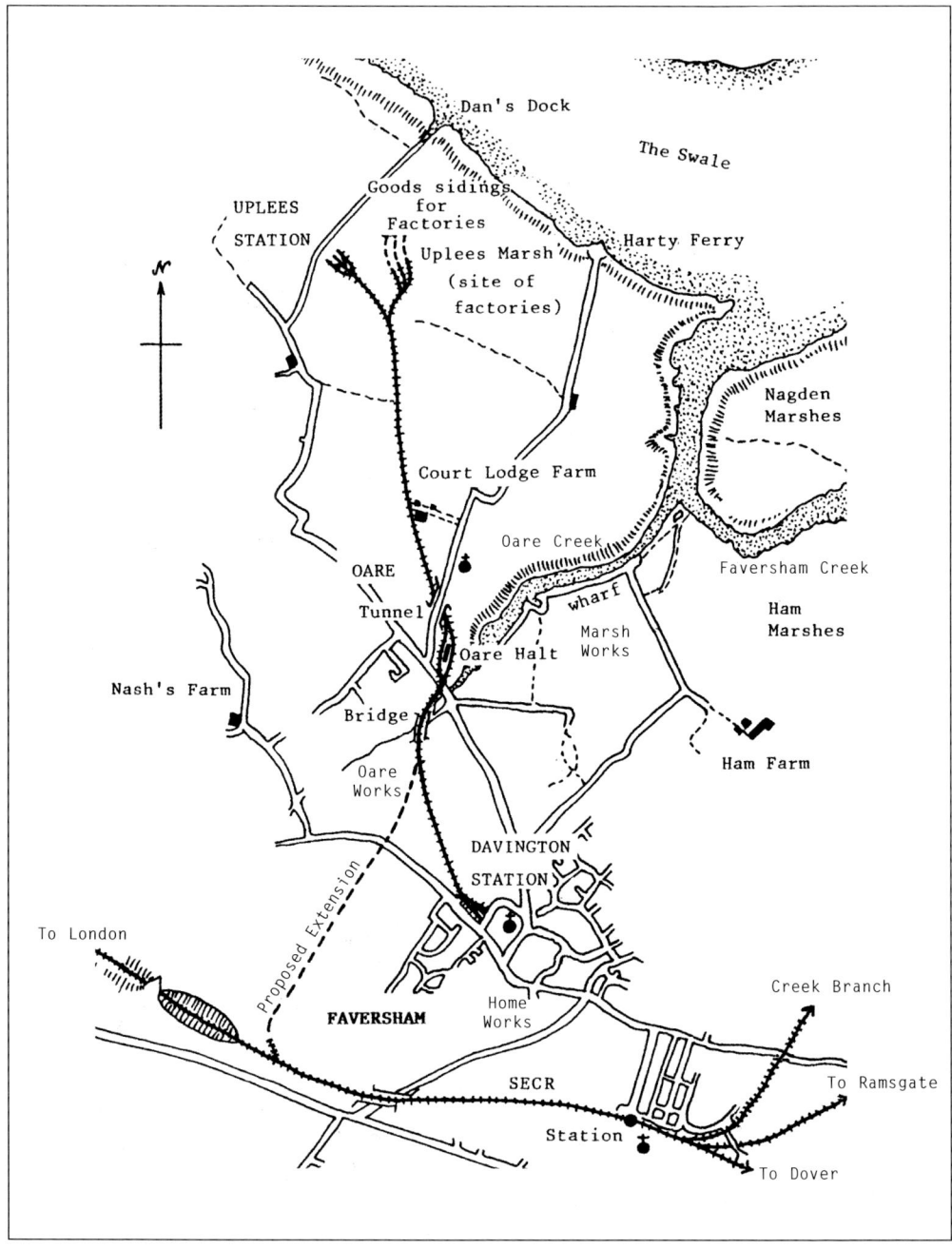

Preface to Second Edition

Much has happened since the first reprint saw the light of day during 1986. Two of the three locomotives, Nos. 2 and 3, were found in Santa Caterina, Brazil, in 1971. Then owned by the Compania Docas Imbituba they were discovered by Roy Christian.

This dock company later donated these engines to the planned railway museum at Tubarao, Santa Caterina. No. 2 was cosmetically restored by the railway works, in Tubarao, but given the number '3' which originally belonged to Manning, Wardle Works No. 1916, the other engine. It was finished in Estrada de Ferro Dona Teresa Cristina (EFDTC) livery and placed on a plinth at the railway works pending completion of the museum, although there is no evidence that this locomotive ever worked on the EFDTC. It was rumoured that the engine might be repatriated to this country but the writer has no evidence to support this.

There was also talk that the Davington Railway would re-open as a tourist line between Oare and Uplees. Bearing in mind the line's proximity to the Sittingbourne & Kemsley Light Railway it could encourage enthusiasts to visit this intriguing area of north-east Kent. The Swale estuary is very beautiful, particularly around Harty Ferry.

Passengers who travelled on the line always referred to it as the Davington Railway but the author has recently learned that the line was officially known as the Faversham Light Railway. This came to light when he received a photograph of carriage No. 7 which was taken by the Gloucester Railway Carriage & Wagon Co. Beside the coach is a plaque stating that the vehicle belonged to the Faversham Light Railway.

It must be understood that the line operated under a cloak of secrecy as is borne out as the pages of this book are turned. The workforce travelling on the railway would have had no idea of the line's official title and as the writer only had the word of the passengers to go on, the book assumed the title *The Davington Light Railway*. History has a habit of re-inventing itself and so this line takes on a new mantle, and the story becomes that much more interesting.

William Kirtley designed the 'M2' class 4-4-0s for the London, Chatham & Dover Railway. No. 643 is seen, in South Eastern & Chatham Railway livery, with Cotton Powder Co. gunpowder vans in the early years of the 20th century. *Fleur de Lis Heritage Centre*

Introduction to First Edition

The entrance to the Cotton Powder Co., Uplees station almost adjoined on the right.
Fleur de Lis Heritage Centre

For unfolding the saga of railway history in Kent the historian has adequately covered such important chapters as the opening of the first public railway in southern England, running between Canterbury and Whitstable, and the feud between the 'South Eastern' (South Eastern Railway) and 'Chatham' (London, Chatham & Dover Railway) companies, the amalgamation of which resulted in a virtual monopoly in the county. The enthusiast may, however, be thwarted in his desire to learn more of the smaller railway systems such as the East Kent Light Railway and the extensive narrow gauge lines belonging to the Bowater Corporation at Sittingbourne, for little has been written of them, and of one exclusive system in particular, a narrow gauge passenger-carrying line which is the subject of this work, nothing at all. This is not surprising bearing in mind the secrecy that surrounded its construction, operation and disposal during its brief existence. The local and county newspapers were not allowed to publish articles or photographs of the railway, and the general public were not permitted to travel on the system.

It is now my privilege to put before my readers for the first time the story of the 'Davington Light Railway' in an endeavour to throw some light on a smaller railway operating in the county of Kent.

The recipe is an unusual one, its ingredients war, gunpowder and people. The railway only had a short life, but on a normal working day more than 1,300 passengers used the line to travel to the Uplees site in the morning and a smilar number returned later in the day. This was the time of the Great War, and here is the history of a railway which grew from war's appetite.

Michael Minter Taylor
1968

Chapter One

Gunpowder:
A Napoleonic Backlash

Davington and Faversham

The parish of Davington (population *circa* 6,000) now mostly lies within the built-up area of Faversham, a market town with a present population approaching 20,000. From prehistoric times this developed around a navigable creek which linked it to the open sea. By medieval times it had become a port significant enough for it to become, as a 'limb' of Dover, a corporate member of the Cinque Ports Confederation.

It came to serve not just its immediate hinterland but parts of the Weald of Kent and, after passage to Fordwich became impossible, Canterbury. For some time it exported more wool than any other English port. From at least the 13th century it also had its own oyster beds and associated exports to the Netherlands in particular.

Because its short route to the sea was indirect, the port's trade suffered after the Canterbury & Whitstable Railway opened in 1830, with a new harbour at Whitstable. However, after the worst of the creek meanders were eliminated in 1843, trade rapidly revived. A further fillip to this came in 1860 when the mile-long Creek branch line, capable - unlike the Canterbury & Whitstable Railway - of taking the heaviest locomotives, linked the port directly with the national rail network.

The *Gilpin* makes slow progress along Faversham Creek. This view illustrates how the creek was used as a maritime/railway interchange, with an unidentified South Eastern & Chatham Railway 4-4-0 visible on the Creek branch. *Fleur de Lis Heritage Centre*

In the later 19th and earlier 20th centuries the creek was teeming with vessels, mainly oyster smacks, sailing barges, and ketches. Lining its banks were a cement factory, grain mills, shipyards and brickfields, producers of the 'London' stock brick which made possible the capital's exponential Victorian expansion. A stone's-throw away were two substantial breweries. The town was a busy industrial one.

Since the first edition of this book appeared all has changed. To all intents and purposes industry has deserted the creek, and with it the trading vessels that berthed alongside its quays. Its main line branch was cut back and lifted in 1962. All trace of it has since gone, apart from its goods shed, a listed building converted into offices.

Of the two breweries, one has closed, its buildings converted into a supermarket, homes and offices. The other, by far the oldest in the United Kingdom, continues to flourish on its site overlooking the creek.

Now, with much new housing along its banks, the creek is coming to look more like a suburban street. However, some maritime trades survive and the hope is that they will continue. This is one of the few ports where traditional coasting vessels - smacks and sailing barges in particular - can still be properly cared for.

The Faversham explosives industry

Faversham was possibly the cradle of the nation's private-sector explosives industry. The first gunpowder mills were at work, on the Home Works not far from the head of the creek, by 1573. Their creation may have been fostered by Faversham Abbey, whose huge church stood close to the waterway until 1538, when it was dissolved by Henry VIII. Most of the mile-long site of the Home Works has been redeveloped for housing, but at its heart survive the Chart Gunpowder Mills, the oldest of their kind in the world. These were rescued from the jaws of the bulldozer by the Faversham Society and then restored by it. Beyond the head of the creek the Works' largest mill-pond, Stonebridge Pond, survives and is now a local beauty spot.

Two other gunpowder factories started later, the Oare and Marsh Works, in the late 17th and late 18th century respectively. Initially all three factories relied on water- or horse-power, but in the 19th century stationary steam engines were installed at all three. In the early 20th century an electricity generating station was provided for the Marsh Works.

Initially the Home and Oare Works sourced two of the three ingredients of gunpowder - charcoal and saltpetre - locally. The third ingredient - sulphur - had to be imported from Sicily, though some may have been sourced from copper at works in Whitstable and Queenborough, on the Isle of Sheppey. From the 18th century saltpetre was also imported, initially from India and later from Chile. Imports for the Home Works arrived at Ordnance Wharf at the head of Faversham Creek, and for the other two at Oare Creek. The finished product

GUNPOWDER: A NAPOLEONIC BACKLASH

Marsh Works' horse-drawn narrow gauge tramway services gunpowder barges on the eastern bank of Oare Creek in 1925. *Fleur de Lis Heritage Centre*

left by both creeks, though by the later 18th century only from Oare Creek, as, unlike Faversham Creek, this was not in a built-up area.

Both the Oare and Marsh Works came to have manumotive railways, and the Marsh Works also had a horse-powered one. All three gunpowder factories closed in 1934, when many of their staff and some of their equipment were moved to Ardeer in Ayshire. The remains of the Oare Works (wholly in the parish of Davington but close to Oare Creek) have been conserved and incorporated into an attractive country park. The buildings of the Marsh Works have mostly been destroyed by aggregates extraction.

Gunpowder is a 'low' explosive, used mainly for its propellant power. High explosives are used mainly for their destructive power. The first, guncotton, was invented in 1846 and first manufactured at Faversham's Marsh Works in the following year. However, following a disastrous explosion the plant closed soon after it opened.

The product was not made in Faversham again till 1873, when the Cotton Powder Co. built a plant at Uplees alongside The Swale, the tidal channel which separates the Isle of Sheppey from mainland Kent. As demand built up, the plant was extended, particularly during World War I. As new high explosives, like tonite (a locally devised product), cordite and TNT, were invented, the plant made them. An extensive network of internal narrow-gauge tramways, on which petrol locomotives ran, was built up.

In 1912 an associated business, the Explosives Loading Co., opened at Uplees a plant adjacent to the Cotton Powder Company's on the west. By the end of the war the two occupied a site whose total area was not far short of that of the City of London's. The number of staff increased dramatically, from 300 before the war, to about 1,500 by the end of 1915.

These two views of the tramway in Marsh Works date from *circa* 1930. Tramway wagons delivered alder or willow to the cylinder house (*above*) for refining into charcoal. In the view below a narrow gauge wagon is seen near the press house. *(Both) Fleur de Lis Heritage Centre*

After closing for gunpowder manufacture in 1934 the Marsh Works site became an aggregates quarry (Ace Sand & Gravel Co.). Petrol locomotives brought raw aggregates in from outside the works site, crossing Oare Road near Oare Creek more or less where the Davington Light Railway had done so. This view shows the terminus at the ballast plant in 1965.
Arthur Percival

Most of the extra staff came from outside Faversham, from towns and villages around it and the Isle of Thanet in particular, as this was well served by main line trains from Faversham. Some women employees were accommodated in temporary hostels in the town itself.

Raw material for the two plants, including coal needed as fuel for their gasworks and generating stations, arrived, and their products reached their destinations, either by Thames sailing barge or, once it had opened, via the Davington Light Railway using road transport, from Faversham main line goods yard. The Cotton Powder Co. had its own fleet of sailing barges, including the *Kent*, built by Goldfinch in Faversham in 1875, the *Surprise*, built in Faversham in 1878, and the United, built in Sittingbourne in 1881. Each factory had its jetty, and the Cotton Powder Company sported a travelling crane.

At the end of hostilities the two factories, and the Davington Light Railway which served them, closed and were dismantled. Most of the site of the Cotton Powder Factory is now the Oare Marshes Nature Reserve, reckoned to be of international importance, particularly for its birdlife. The rest of its site, and that of the Explosives Loading Company, is now grazing land.*

---

* The full story of the town's explosives industry is told in *The Faversham Gunpowder Industry and its Development*, (Faversham Papers No. 4, Third Edition, 1986) also by Arthur Percival and available from the Heritage Centre. Other relevant studies, all in the Faversham Papers series and available from the Heritage Centre are:

27	Gunpowder: Terminology and Incorporation (1986) by Edward Patterson
39	Oare Gunpowder Works (1994) by Wayne Cocroft
42	Gunpowder Manufacture at Faversham (1995) by Edward Patterson
58	Guns, Gunpowder & Saltpetre by Edward Patterson
84	Faversham Gunpowder Personnel Register 1573-1840 by Raymond Godfrey & Arthur Percival
103-105	Faversham Explosives Personnel Register 1841-1934 by John Breeze

The north-eastern area of the Cotton Powder Co. works. This view gives an idea of the nature and size of the plant, and shows quite a few works railway lines.
Fleur de Lis Heritage Centre

Below: A diagrammatic plan of the layout of the Cotton Powder Co. works. This has been based on a sketch, drawn from memory, by Syd Twist who worked at the plant.

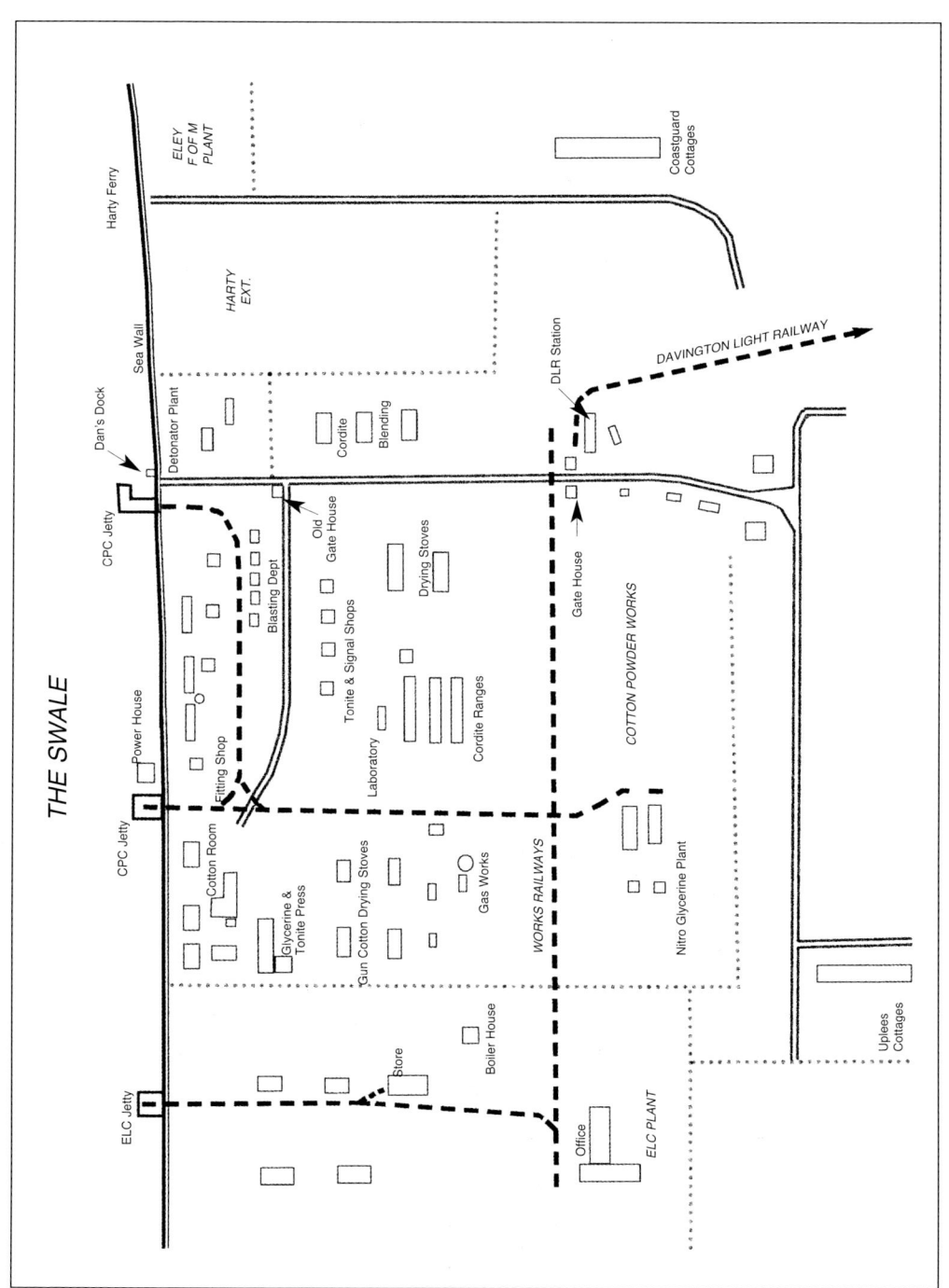

Davington

Davington, the parish which gave its name to the railway, did not become part of the Borough of Faversham (since 1974 merged with other authorities to form the Borough of Swale) until 1935. When the railway was built it had few inhabitants. Its rapid growth as a suburb of the town did not start till the 1960s.

In 1916 its nucleus, on a plateau rising in parts quite sharply 50 ft above lower ground around it, consisted of the austere Norman nave and west tower of its Priory founded in 1153; the remains of the adjacent nuns' quarters, then and now a small country house; Davington Court, a 17th century manor house then serving as a farmhouse; Priory Row, a long mid-19th-century terrace of respectable houses known locally, for reasons unknown, as the 'Forty Thieves'; and one or two other dwellings in Priory Road, which skirted the Priory.

West of this, nearly a mile away, were the Oare Gunpowder Works and then Bysing Wood, on a much higher ridge. Between the nucleus and the Oare Works was rich low-lying loamlands which had once been used for farming. Since the later 19th century, however, these had been worked as brickfields, with 'London' stocks being fired not in kilns but in open-air 'clamps'. One at least had closed shortly before the Davington Light Railway opened. It was two of these brickfields that the line crossed to reach its intermediate station at the head of Oare Creek.

Priory Row circa 1930. No. 1 Priory Row (*just out of view to the right of the shop*) now bears a blue plaque. In the 1950s and 1960s it was the home of the distinguished architect W. Godfrey Allen. Improbably, it was here that he did all the plans for the restoration of London's St Paul's Cathedral after World War II, and later for that of the Sheldonian Theatre in Oxford. *Fleur de Lis Heritage Centre*

Its Davington terminus lay at the foot of the Davington Plateau, a small part of which had to be excavated to make room for it. On the east it was picturesquely overlooked by Priory Road and part of the grounds of Davington Priory. After the line closed the station site remained vacant, or in desultory use for agricultural and other purposes.

Eventually in the 1980s it became the site of a small cul-de-sac housing development. At the suggestion of the Faversham Society, this was named Admiralty Close, because the railway had been created and managed by the Admiralty, which had requisitioned the high explosives factories it served for the duration of World War I.

On 2nd April, 1916, not long before the Davington Light Railway opened, a disastrous explosion - the worst in the history of the UK explosives industry - occurred at the Explosives Loading Co. plant. It left at least 108 dead and many more injured, some very seriously. Most of the dead were buried in a mass grave in Faversham Cemetery. A full account of the disaster, by Arthur Percival, is available from the Faversham Society at its Fleur de Lis Heritage Centre in Preston Street, in the town centre.

Events leading up to the opening of the Davington Light Railway

The first years of World War I saw the thousands of workers employed in the gunpowder factories on the Uplees Marshes finding their own way to and from the sites. But as 1916 proved to be a very wet year and the hard slog from Faversham across muddy fields to work hazardous to health and productivity in this vital phase of the war, a deputation representing the workers requested a meeting with their employers to discuss possible transport facilities. The matter was soon put in hand and in a very short space of time motor coaches arrived on the scene.

Twenty vehicles were supplied, having solid wheels and rollback hoods. Although inadequate for the task they did give the workers a better deal in more than one respect, for, besides the routine service, they could even hire these coaches for Saturday night sorties to nearby places such as Chatham.

It was soon apparent that a more efficient transport system must be provided, as the factories on the marshes were expanding and even more people had to be carried in each direction daily. The General Workers Union had kept a close watch on this growing problem from their headquarters in the Limes Hotel, Preston Street, Faversham. Numerous meetings were called and it must be recognised that it was through their efforts the Davington Light Railway was born.

Emergency Powers had to be obtained to enable the main railway line to cross the Davington to Oare road and pass beneath the Oare/Harty Ferry road. It is generally understood that Lloyd George, Prime Minister at the time, was wholeheartedly in favour of the scheme and there is no doubt that his approval helped to expedite the matter through the relevant Government Department and bring about speedy legislation.

The contract for the construction of the railway was entrusted to Messrs Topham, Jones & Railton Ltd, a firm of civil engineering contractors based in south Wales who specialized in dockyard and harbour work and had previously undertaken much work for the Admiralty at home and abroad. As the new railway would connect with the existing internal narrow gauge railway systems of the various explosives factories the same unusual track gauge of 3 ft 3 in. was used. To assist in the railway construction the contractors brought in their own locomotive, a small four-coupled Bagnall tank. Construction commenced in April or May 1916 and the finished light railway was formally opened to both passenger and goods traffic in November 1916. However, it appears that in practice the railway was operating some sort of service before this for a photograph of Davington station dated 6th October, 1916 clearly shows workers disembarking from a short two-coach passenger train headed by the contractor's Bagnall locomotive. This had presumably been pressed into passenger use although the first of the three Manning, Wardle 0-6-0ST had arrived a few days earlier.

Davington station before the official opening, showing a worker's train hauled by a contractor's locomotive, a Bagnall 0-4-0WT. *Andrew Neale Collection*

Chapter Two

The Railway

The route described

Davington station lay tucked under the summit of Dark Hill, the buffer stops lying immediately beneath Priory Road. To obtain access to the station a flight of steps dropped down from the Bysing Wood Road on to one of two platforms. At the top of the stairs was located the ticket office. The platforms at Davington were approximately 2 ft high and surfaced with ash. Paraffin lamp standards adorned the platforms, but the lamps were seldom lit owing to blackout regulations.

The gauge was 3 ft 3 in. and the main line rail was 60 lb. per yard laid on sleepers spaced out at approximately 12 per 30 ft of rail. The gauge was chosen as the builders of the line were the same contractors who built the metre gauge line in Gibraltar dockyard at the turn of the 19th/20th centuries and the Bagnall locomotive shown in the photograph, taken before opening, almost certainly came from this source. The rail was seated into chairs which, in turn, were fastened down to wooden sleepers, shipped to Uplees by some of the numerous Thames sailing barges operating in the estuary at that time. Some of the track was of a lighter nature and wooden keys were used to stop the rails spreading outwards.

The single line was tripled at Davington, the centre track going into the engine shed hard up against the side of the hill. This feature enabled a locomotive to run-round its train at the finish of a journey by using one of the two links to get back on to the centre track and the other spur to join up with its train again ready for the next working as no turntable was available.

The engine shed was a large wooden structure with ample room for the three locomotives. An inspection pit ran its entire length. Immediately in front of the big double doors on the right-hand side of the centre track, if one was looking toward Oare, stood the water tank beside which was one of three storage sheds.

Proceeding along the nearest of the three railway lines in a westerly direction, after crossing over the points which would have given access to the centre line, and traversing some 300 yards of track, the goods shed was reached at the end of this short siding. This was of cantilever construction with a small travelling overhead crane used for lifting the loaded mines from the railway trucks on to the lorries parked at right angles to the railway line. There was also a fixed crane mounted on three concrete bases.

This then was the layout of Davington station and goods yard. After leaving the station and sidings on the left, the line curved away to the right towards the village of Oare. The track was laid on Thanet Beds resting on an eroded chalk surface. These earth deposits are composed of, in the main, marine sands, fossilferous sandy clays, and flints. To lay the track a thin layer of this soil,

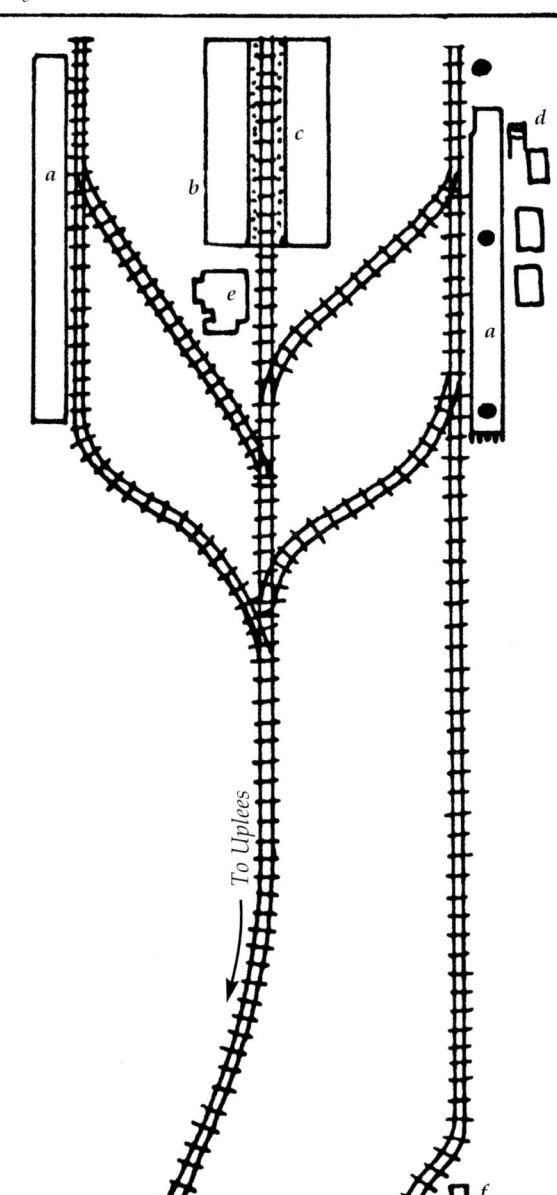

which could be loosely termed loam, was scooped off to reveal flints which constituted the bed on which the sleepers were laid.

The track between Davington and Oare traverses almost level ground although there is a very gradual drop to Oare Halt, the lowest point on the line being a few feet above sea-level. Between these two stopping places it was planned to have a further line branching off to the left, past what used to be the workhouse, leading to the London to Dover railway line of the South Eastern & Chatham Railway (SECR). This would have enabled explosives to be carried from the factories at Uplees straight to the standard gauge line, at a point approximately a mile west of Faversham station, where the freight would have been speedily dispatched to the battlefields of Flanders far more effectively than by the use of lorries mentioned earlier. However, nothing came of this scheme and it died a natural death.

Before reaching Oare the stream leading into Oare Creek had to be crossed. The bridge was of simple construction, wooden piles being driven into the bed of the rivulet and set in concrete. The single span was also of wood and was without handrails or guards. Immediately after traversing the bridge the Davington/Uplees road had to be crossed. A level crossing controlled the traffic which was operated by the crossing keeper who watched over his job from a hut nearby. Once across the road Oare Halt was but a few yards away. This meagre stopping place consisted solely of a raised wooden platform situated on the Oare Creek side of the railway line. There were no station buildings or anywhere to shelter if adverse weather conditions prevailed. It was at this point, however, that an emergency loop had thoughtfully been provided by the contractors. This ran behind the platform and enabled a locomotive with four carriages to pass a similarly composed train which had stopped at the Halt. This was, in fact, the only crossing place on this single line.

After leaving Oare the line began a slight climb which culminated at Court Lodge Farm 50 ft above sea-level, the highest point on the line. On the right-hand side, proceeding towards Uplees, the passenger would have a fine view of some 20 or so Thames sailing barges, many of which would be employed loading explosives. On the left, the village of Oare situated on higher ground. A cluster of whitewashed cottages dominated by two inns and a church. The railway track cut across the meadowland beneath the settlement, but as the land provided pasture for cattle this part of the line was fenced in, although there was a private crossing to allow cattle and farmhands to proceed from the pasture to the two dairies in the village.

Just beyond this private crossing was the major engineering work on the railway, the tunnel cutting beneath the Oare/Harty Ferry road halfway between Oare Halt and Court Lodge Farm.

The dimensions were as follows:

Length	80 ft	6 in.
Width	11 ft	2 in.
Height (from floor to top of sides)	10 ft	4 in.
Height (from floor to top of dome)	12 ft	4 in.

The end of the line at Uplees, with a train waiting in the station. *Arthur Percival*

A close-up of Uplees station platform. *Arthur Percival*

The outer portals were faced in concrete bearing the inscription '1916', the date of the opening of the railway. Messrs Topham Jones and Railton built this underpass and were also responsible for the entire works on the railway, besides carrying out many other contracts for the Admiralty, including an extension to the Gibraltar Dockyard in about 1900. This construction company used a Bagnall locomotive, which was probably one from its Gibraltar contract, and can be seen in one of the accompanying photographs. This engine had cylinders measuring 8 in. x 12 in. and driving wheels $24\frac{1}{2}$ in. in diameter, and was built in the 1890s. Inside the tunnel four recesses (two each side) were provided for the protection of gangers who may have been working on the system during operating hours.

After leaving the tunnel the line continued its steady climb to Court Lodge Farm before dropping down on to the Harty and Uplees Marshes. The line from here on was laid on alluvium, which was not liable to flooding owing to the sea wall that enclosed the marsh.

Approximately a quarter of a mile from the terminus a branch line swung away to the right taking the goods traffic towards the factories. This line quickly divided into three and after a very short distance made end-on connections with the factory railway system. The railway operating within the industrial area was of the same guage of 3 ft 3 in. but the rails were in 14 and 20 lb. per yard and consequently the main line locomotives were not allowed to work over the factory lines. Throughout this minor system wooden keys were used to stop the rails spreading outwards, instead of the more conventional methods.

The main line itself continued past ballast tips into Uplees station. Once again the line split into three and a similar platform and track layout was adopted as at Davington, with a water tank situated on the left of the centre track close to the buffers. Close by the railway station stood two cottages. One was the factory gatekeeper's home, the other the telephone exchange. These buildings, however, each served a dual purpose. Men and women leaving the trains or factories were searched for combustible materials, the men using the gatekeeper's cottage, women the telephone exchange.

So ends the description of the route and now we must proceed to aspects relating to the operation of this gunpowder line.

Staff

The Davington Light operated with the minimum of staff. The Admiralty employed two station masters, Mr Foreman at Davington and a Mr Geater who supervised affairs in the Uplees area. Perhaps it would be more correct to say that they were station foremen; anyway in them lay the responsibility of day-to-day working on the system. Between them they supervised goods and passenger timings, sold and collected the railway tickets besides covering any emergency which might arise. If for instance an air-raid alert was sounded

The Davington terminus photographed in a quiet period showing 12 curtained open carriages. Note the Admiralty freight wagon bottom right. *Arthur Percival*

Workers climbing the hill into Oare village; the railway halt was situated behind the photographer, beside Oare Creek. *Fleur de Lis Heritage Centre*

during the working hours employees at the factories were instructed to congregate on the Uplees station platforms and await the trains. Such an emergency would be handled by the station masters who would have to clear the main line of goods traffic, hurriedly make up three train sets with their engines, which may have been employed on goods work at the time of the alert, and dispatch them to Uplees station with the minimum of delay.

A word or two on the composition of the trains would not be out of place at this juncture. Three locomotives were employed on the main line railway, to handle both passenger and freight workings. The passenger trains normally operated early in the morning, to get the workers to the factories, and in the evening to bring them back to Davington. In between these two rush periods, the same engines were occupied on goods workings, the last freight train of the day always leaving Uplees at 3.30 pm. The three train sets referred to previously were each made up of four carriages and a description of these will follow later.

Reverting to the staff employed on the railway, reference must now be made to the three engine drivers. William Davies was first choice pilot, his immediate colleague being William Moore. There is some doubt as to the third driver, but it was thought to be a Mr Saunders who emigrated to Canada after World War I. No information is to hand giving the names of the firemen, who presumably were able to take over driving duties should one or other of the senior men be ill.

At Oare a Mr Philpott and Mr Davis were employed to look after the level crossing and signalling arrangements such as existed on the line. In fact the only signals were located at Oare and consisted of the human arm. The signalman was provided with red and green flags during daylight hours and similar coloured lamps at night, his only other tool being the key. As the track was single throughout, with the exception of the Oare Halt loop, the engine driver approaching Oare would sound his whistle and start slowing. This would enable the signalman to hand over the key or token to the driver when he passed. Naturally the token would be handed over only if the section Oare Halt/Uplees or Oare Halt/Davington was clear.

No details exist of the guards, engine cleaners or greasers who worked on the railway but it may be considered somewhat surprising that quite a number of those employed on the Davington Light Railway came from the South Eastern & Chatham Railway.

Finally it should be recorded that no official uniform was issued to the railway employees.

Passengers disembark from the train in August 1917.
The Faversham Society

Passengers leaving a 'Ladies only' train at Davington. This is the photograph that started my research in the railway. It should never have been taken in view of the secret nature of the line.
The Faversham Society

The timetable

Mondays to Fridays		am	am	am	am	am	am	am
Davington	dep.	6.10	6.30	6.50	7.10	7.30	7.50	8.10
Oare Halt	arr.	6.14	6.34	6.54	7.14	7.34	7.52	8.14
	dep.	6.16	6.36	6.56	7.16	7.36	7.54	8.16
Uplees (Harty)	arr.	6.20	6.40	7.00	7.20	7.40	8.00	8.20

Mondays to Fridays		pm	pm	pm	pm	pm	pm	pm
Uplees (Harty)	dep.	5.10	5.30	5.50	6.10	6.30	6.50	7.10
Oare Halt	arr.	5.14	5.34	5.54	6.14	6.34	6.54	7.14
	dep.	5.16	5.36	5.56	6.16	6.36	6.56	7.16
Davington	arr.	5.20	5.40	6.00	6.20	6.40	7.00	7.20

Although extreme care has been taken in compiling this timetable it must be emphasised that there may be errors. It is understood that no official timetable was issued for use by the gunpowder workers and clerical staff at the factories, and as a result the timings shown have been obtained by the author's personal approach to former employees who travelled on the railway. The final result is a compilation of their information.

Extra trains were run outside these hours mainly for shift workers who helped to keep the factories going during the hours of darkness and over the weekends. Trains were also timetabled to run on Saturday mornings, but the last journey from Uplees to Davington was 2 pm; after that time anyone who was left behind had to walk.

An unusual feature of the railway was that many of the trains were for the sole occupancy of either men or women. (It should be noted that the number of women employees at the gunpowder factories was at least equal to that of the men if not greater.) As a result the ladies travelled in the later trains from Davington in the morning and by the first journeys leaving Uplees in the evening. This arrangement gave a little extra time to these womenfolk to tend to their domestic chores.

As many as 40 or 50 people used to endeavour to board the trains at Oare. A wait at this draughty outpost was not at all uncommon as many trains would have left Davington full and no standing was allowed. It must have been bitterly cold in winter with a north-east wind blowing straight off the North Sea, or the German Ocean as it was called prior to the outbreak of hostilities.

Fares and tickets

There was only one fare and that was 2d. return. The tickets were originally of white card with a tuppenny motif stamped on them. These were later superseded by green and fawn cardboard tickets used on alternate days. The printing was black giving the number, day of the week on which the ticket was issued and details of the journey.

Thought to be the only DLR ticket still in existence (outward half only).

It was suggested that special weekend tickets be issued by the SECR to enable the gunpowder workers, some of whom came long distances to work on the munitions, to reach their homes regularly and at the same time saving the men from financial worries. Unfortunately the outcome of this idea is unknown.

Whilst on the subject of main line railways readers may be interested to know that the Admiralty were concerned with the connections the SECR offered munitions workers travelling to Faversham from the Isle of Thanet. As it was approximately a mile from Faversham station to the light railway terminus at Davington it was essential that sufficient time was given to the workers to get from one to the other.

A poor quality image of one of the three Manning, Wardle engines hauling a Gloucester Railway Carriage & Wagon Co. toastrack carriage. *Fleur de Lis Heritage Centre*

Chapter Three

Rolling Stock

Contractor's locomotives

As mentioned earlier Topham, Jones & Railton employed their own locomotive in the construction of the line. This was a four-coupled Bagnall fitted with an inverted saddle tank, i.e. the saddle tank passed beneath the boiler giving an impression of two separate small side tanks at the front of the locomotive although in reality they were one. Fitted with outside cylinders of 8½ inches bore and 12 inch stroke and driving wheels of 24½ inches diameter Bagnall No. 1474 was the last of eight similar locomotives (Nos. 1467 to 1474) supplied between December 1895 and February 1896 to the Admiralty for use at Gibraltar dockyard. They were passed on to Topham, Jones & Railton in 1899 for use on their large construction contract there which lasted until 1906.

Bagnall 1474 then returned to England to assist in the construction of the Ocean Dock at Southampton for the London & South Western Railway, a job that was completed in 1911. It is then presumed to have been returned to the owner's plant depot at Crymlyn Burrows, Swansea to await further work. The next trace was on 23rd March, 1916 when spares were ordered from Bagnall, when presumably it was being made ready for service at Davington. Further spares were ordered on 4th June, 1917 to be sent direct to Davington. After this there is no definite trace. However, in the absence of any other job for it the locomotive may well have gone back to Swansea. At any rate in December 1919 an auction of surplus plant at Crymlyn Barrows to be held on 7th January, 1920 included an 'eight inch metre gauge Bagnall' which was probably No. 1474. It may well not have sold for a further auction on 22nd April, 1924 included 'standard and metre gauge locomotives' after which no more is known. Yet another auction sale of surplus locomotives on 10th April, 1926 did not mention any metre gauge ones so it must be presumed that the little Bagnall had been sold for scrap or further use by then.

Main line locomotives

To work the Davington Light Railway Messrs Topham, Jones & Railton placed an order with Manning, Wardle in Leeds on 19th May, 1916 for three 0-6-0ST of 3 ft 3 in. gauge. Like most narrow gauge locomotives built by Manning, Wardle these were described by them as 'Specials' as they were a one-off design specific to this order, and not one of the maker's large range of standard types although inevitably many of their components were to drawings and patterns already produced for previous locomotives. As can be seen from the details below all three were built to a most modern and somewhat lavish design.

THE DAVINGTON LIGHT RAILWAY

Maker's photograph of No. 3.　　　　　　　　　　*Mr Horsman, Hunslet Engine Co.*

Locomotive No. 3 in service.　　　　　　　　　　　　　　*Provenance Unknown*

Manning, Wardle allocated their order No. 74800 for the job with the three 0-6-0STs carrying builder's Nos. 1914 to 1916 respectively together with the railway running Nos. 1, 2 and 3 in 6 inch brass numerals on the coal bunker side. They were fitted with outside cylinders of 9 in. bore by 14 in. stroke with six-coupled wheels of 2 ft 9 in. diameter on a rigid wheelbase of 8 ft 3 in. The boilers were of best mild steel pressed to a working pressure of 160 psi with a steel firebox and a total heating surface of 242 sq. ft made up of 30 sq. ft in the firebox and the balance via 58 two-inch outside diameter lap welded iron tubes. The fire grate area was 4.5 sq. ft, saddle tank capacity 300 gallons and in view of the hazardous nature of the line's traffic spark arrestors were fitted both to the top of the chimney and in the smoke box. All three were fitted with both steam and handbrakes, rail washing gear, two central buffing and draw gears, one higher and one lower (presumably for working both main line and internal factory wagons), two Manning No. 4 injectors but no feed pump and lubrication via a Roscoe No. 2 size displacement lubricator.

The order specified a livery of battleship grey with red buffer beams and white lining but for whatever reason it appears that in reality black, not white, lining was actually applied. The promised delivery for all three locomotives was the 23rd August, 1916 but in the event pressure of other work meant all three were somewhat late being sent away by the builder on 30th September, (No. 1), 23rd October (No. 2) and finally No. 3 on 11th November.

Factory engines

To cope with the anticipated increase in production in early 1914 it was decided that a locomotive was needed for the internal factory railways. As no suitable internal combustion locomotive was available in Britain an order was placed with the German firm of Deutz. Deutz had been building a range of small narrow gauge petrol/paraffin locomotives for some time and had already sold several to British customers. Accordingly the Cotton Powder Co. ordered one of their 'Model XII' 10 hp four-wheeled locomotives and Deutz Works No. 1529 was shipped to Faversham on 6th June, 1914. The sale proved to be a most unfortunate one for the German firm as due to the outbreak of war between Britain and Germany at the beginning of August it was never actually paid for.

Adding insult to injury, by the following year the little Deutz was overwhelmed by the level of traffic and further similar locomotives were obviously needed. To resolve the problem the Admiralty turned to Ruston, Proctor & Co. Ltd of Lincoln, then one of Britain's most experienced builders of oil engines. The Admiralty placed an order for a further locomotive stating that 'the engine is to be the equal in every respect to the Otto Deutz engine now being used and capable of doing the same work'.

Ruston, Proctor produced a 10 hp locomotive, their No. 50823, delivering it on 7th June, 1915. It was remarkably similar in appearance and design to the Deutz locomotive and was fitted with a Ruston's single-cylinder water-cooled

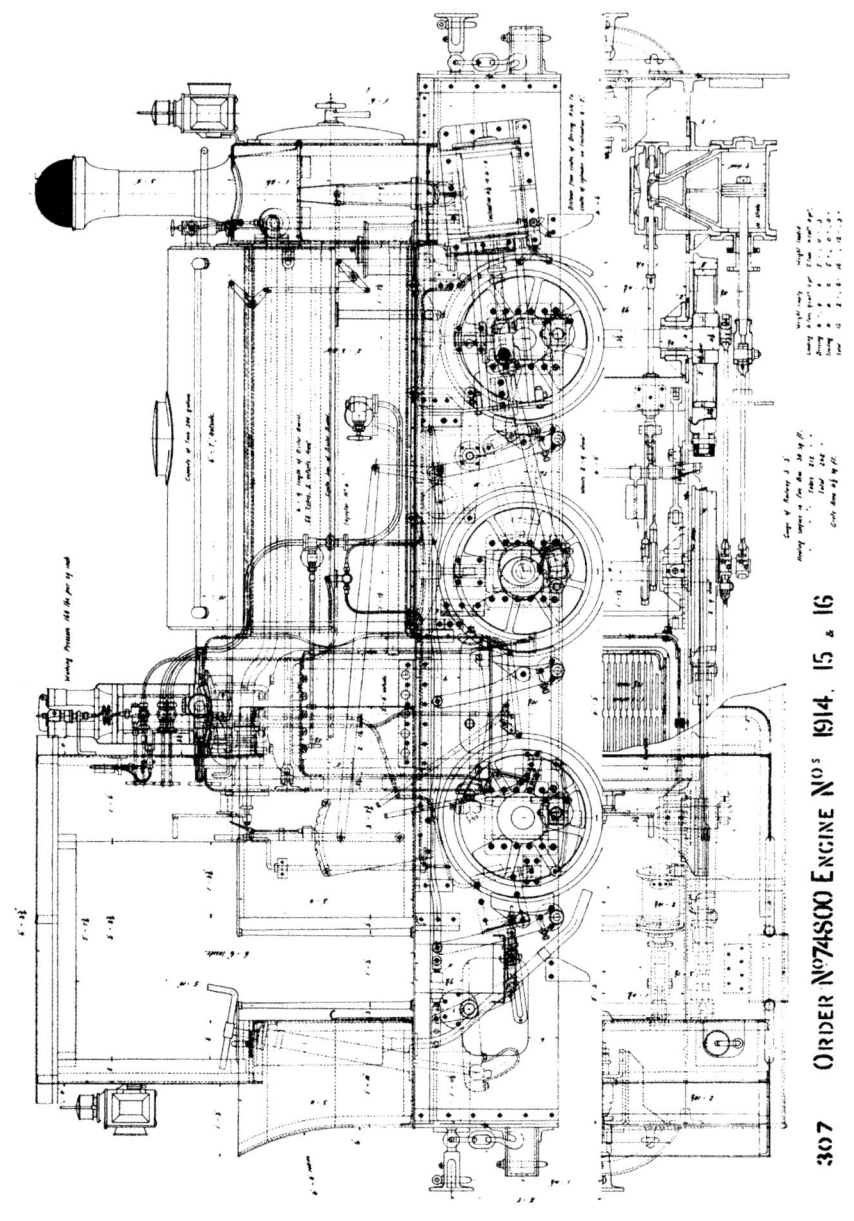

307 Order No 74800 Engines Nos 1914, 15 & 16

Side elevation of the Manning, Wardle engines.

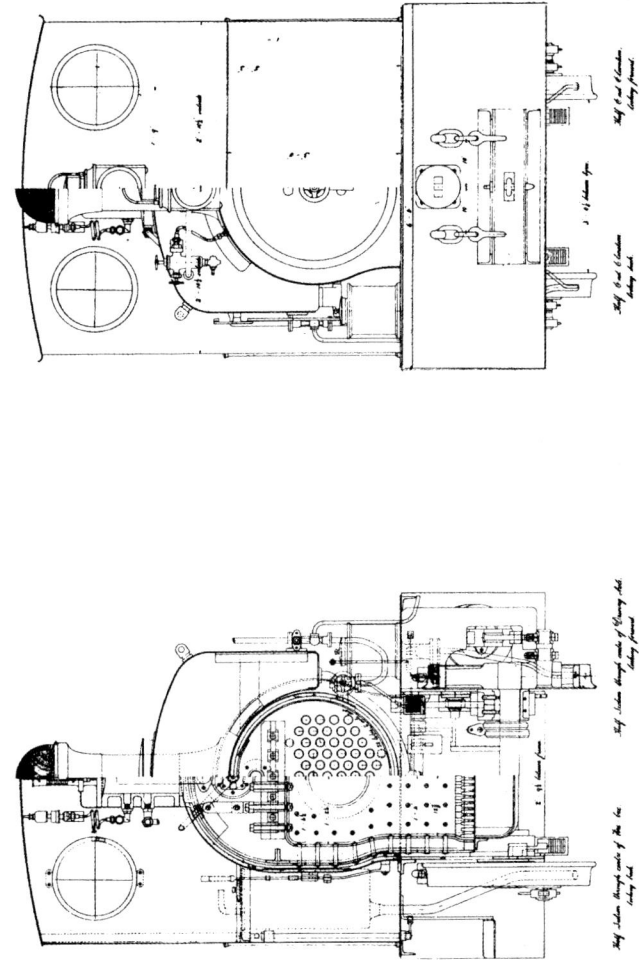

End elevation of the Manning, Wardle engines.

Ruston, Proctor factory engine at the gasworks, Uplees. *Provenance Unknown*

Ruston, Proctor No. 51168 at Blackpool china clay pit, Trewoon, St Austell on 25th July, 1956. It never saw use here as railway track was never laid, the intention had been to connect two pits by rail via a tunnel. *Maurice Dart*

No. 51168 at Blackpool china clay pit on 24th November, 1956. The locomotive was dumped behind a workshop. *Maurice Dart*

For many years the Ruston, Proctor at Blackpool china clay works was believed to be No. 50823, and that number is seen clearly displayed on the cabside here at the Vale of Rheidol in September 2002. It was only during restoration that the true identity of the locomotive, No. 51168, was discovered. *Robin J. Parkinson*

No. 51168 at the Vale of Rheidol Railway, Aberystwyth in September 2002. *Robin J. Parkinson*

No. 51168, at Allen Civil's works, nears complete restoration. *Robin J. Parkinson*

engine transversely mounted as in the Deutz. Its immediate success prompted orders for two more, Ruston No. 50861 going to join its predecessor on the 13th July and Ruston No. 50878 to the Explosives Loading Co. on 28th July. Two more similar locomotives, Ruston's Nos. 51168 and 51207 were delivered to the Cotton Powder Co. on the 13th and 27th March the following year.

These oil locomotives were designated the 'ZLH' class and a similar 20 hp locomotive using a twin-cylinder engine but with the wheels mounted inside the frames was designated the 'ZLHD'. Ruston, Proctor (Ruston & Hornsby Ltd from April 1918) built several more 'ZLH' locomotives of various gauges for other Admiralty armament depots during the Great War and built further examples up to 1930. They were the predecessors for their very successful small diesel locomotives built in quantity from 1931 which led to Ruston becoming the largest manufacturer of such locomotives in Britain.

The final locomotive to work in the explosives factories was another small petrol locomotive. It was built by Baguley Cars Ltd of Burton-on-Trent who had recently begun building small petrol locomotives. The War Office ordered three of what would be a new standard 10 hp design, two of 600 mm gauge for service in France and a third of 3 ft 3 in. gauge for the Explosives Loading Co. at Uplees. Baguley No. 676 was ordered on 4th November, 1915 and delivered to Faversham on 12th June the following year. Like its narrower gauge sisters it somewhat resembled a small steam locomotive with the four driving wheels outside the frames coupled by side rods, a jack shaft at the rear and its two-cylinder Baguley engine and transmission concealed under a neat circular cowling which together with the similar water cooling tank gave the appearance of a steam locomotive boiler.

They were used for pulling the concentrated acid bogie, which contained nitric acid, from the acid plant to the nitroglycerine plant, besides hauling loads of six to eight tipper trucks loaded with coal from the jetty on the river Swale to the gasworks located on the factory site. For performing this task an engine driver could expect to earn £3 7s. a week.

Carriages

This little railway was allocated 12 toastrack type passenger coaches. As mentioned earlier each locomotive had charge of four coaches and the railway adopted the system permanently dividing the stock into three sets, two of which operated the line, the third being held in reserve ready to fill the breach in the case of a breakdown. The dimensions were:

Length over headstocks	28 ft 3 in.
Width over corner pillars	6 ft 4½ in.
Length over buffers	30 ft 3 in.
Width overall	7 ft 4 in.
Centres of bogies	19 ft 3 in.
Weight	6 tons 11 cwt 1 quarter

Two views of Baguley petrol locomotive No. 676 taken in Baguley's works yard at Burton-on-Trent. *(Both) Baguley-Drewry Archive Collection*

Each carriage was constructed of wood with iron frames mounted on two four-wheel bogies. A hand brake was fitted in every case. Tarpaulins were fitted to provide protection in bad weather, and being of greenish hue provided a contrast with the battleship grey of the coaching stock. Inside wooden slatted seats were fitted, back to back, capable of seating four passengers each side, giving a coach capacity of 48 persons.

A strict rule forbade passengers standing in the carriage and before the trains left the terminus stations guards would check on this bye law and draw aside the tarpaulins to make absolutely sure that no persons were transgressing. The poor guards got short shrift from the workers and were usually told to get out and close the door, a little ironical bearing in mind that toastrack carriages have neither doors nor windows.

These coaches were built to a high standard by the Gloucester Railway Carriage & Wagon Co. Ltd. A photograph in the author's possession depicts carriage No. 7, built in July 1916 and given order No. 3089, proves the point. The passengers may have complained about the hard wooden seats but the service provided was infinitely better than trudging across muddy fields as had been the case prior to the opening of this Admiralty railway.

Wagons

Only two types of vehicle were used on the main line railway and these were flat and high-sided wagons. The flats were used for the carriage of mines, whilst the deep trucks conveyed bombs, shells, gun cotton, paste, cordite, acid besides many other miscellaneous items. (Gun cotton is an explosive prepared from saturating cotton with nitric acid.) The acid was bottled and encased in straw. Extensive use was made of tarpaulins.

All wagons were of wooden construction with iron frames and stiffeners up the sides. After arrival on the Davington Light Railway extensive safety modifications were embodied into all the rolling stock employed in the conveying of explosives. Leather covers were placed over all bolt heads and some wagons had an additional wooden interior, which could be termed a cofferdam, fastened by means of bronze and copper nails. These precautions were taken to ensure that all metal was sheathed to obviate any danger of sparking.

These wagons were all interchangeable for working over the main line or the factory lines; but in addition to the stock mentioned above there were two types of wagon used exclusively on the factory system to which brief mention has already been made. They were the coal tipper trucks and the concentrated acid bogie. The tipper trucks were of 1 ton tare and capable of carrying either 40 or 80 cu. ft each. (These figures were given independently to the author who has no means of verifying which is correct.) No details are known of the acid bogie. Once again the livery employed was battleship grey with black lining. Each wagon side was boxed out in two hollow black squares and must have looked rather smart when new. Despite the hazardous nature of their cargoes the wagons came through the war unscathed, possibly because of the extensive precautions taken to prevent accident. No major fault could be found, with one probable exception: the tipper trucks with their small dimensions would be difficult to tip owing to their broad wheelbase.

The Gloucester Carriage & Wagon Company's official photograph of Davington's bogie carriage No. 7. *The British Overseas Railways Historical Trust*

Chapter Four

Closure

The life of the Davington Light Railway could be counted in months as soon as the Armistice had been declared. Production at the factories slowed to a mere trickle, and the workers gradually returned to their peace-time occupations, although a few remained to help with the manufacture of the small amount of explosives needed. A first auction of surplus factory plant was held by Messrs Fuller, Horsey on behalf of the Cotton Powder Co. in March 1919 and this included both the Baguley petrol locomotive and 'trucks', probably some of side tipping coal wagons. The locomotive obviously failed to sell as it was included in a second sale the following September together with the Ruston, Proctor paraffin locomotive No. 50878. They presumably found buyers as no more was heard of them.

By 1920 all the factories had closed and arrangements were made to sell both their contents and the railway by auction. On 14th September, 1921 Messrs Geering & Colyer offered for sale most of the Davington Light Railway including the four remaining Ruston, Proctor petrol/paraffin locomotives, 72 trucks, 6 coaches and 12,000 yards of track while at a second auction on 27th September held on behalf of the liquidators of the Cotton Powder Factory, Fuller Horsey offered among much other plant the Deutz paraffin locomotive. The three Manning, Wardle 0-6-0STs were not included in either auction as it would seem they were sold soon after the closure in 1920 to Messrs J.I. Thorneycroft Ltd who sent them back to the maker's works in Leeds for overhaul. No. 3 (Works No. 1916) was given a general repair and packed ready for shipment in December 1920. The other two were left until Thorneycroft had found a buyer for them all, after which they were given a complete overhaul in September 1921 which included the fitting of new copper fireboxes and brass tubes.

Only one Ruston, Proctor locomotive, Works No. 51168, was sold at the 1921 auction being purchased by English Clays, Lovering & Pochin Ltd for their Blackpool China Clay Works at St Austell in Cornwall. For whatever reason it was never put to work, lying outside in an increasingly decrepit state for over 40 years, until rescued for preservation by Richard Morris in October 1964 and moved to his home near Exeter, then subsequently to Longfield in Kent (where the author was invited to view the locomotive) and then ultimately becoming a part of the display of Mr Morris's narrow gauge locomotive collection at the former Oakley slate quarry at Blaenau Ffestiniog in North Wales. On the dissolution of that collection at the end of 1997 it was purchased by the Phyllis Rampton Trust and meticulously restored by the late Allen Civil and is now on display at the Vale of Rheidol Railway at Aberystwyth.

The fate of the other three Ruston, Proctor locomotives is unclear. They were included in yet another auction at Harty Ferry on 4th April, 1922 when one of them presumably sold and the other two subsequently moved to Chatham dockyard for storage, to be included in one more auction held on 8th July, 1924 when all further trace is lost.

Oare Church Road tunnel in August 1988. *Arthur Percival*

Davington Light Railway formation at Oare Court Lodge looking north-west in October 2010.
Arthur Percival

CLOSURE

The only remains of the line itself between Uplees and Oare tunnel could best be detected from an aeroplane. From ground level little can be seen, only the concrete water tank base at Uplees together with long shallow grass banks which were once the platforms of this terminus station. A heap of ballast lies where it was dumped all those years before at the point where the factory branch leaves the main line.

Only the major engineering work of the line remains immutable as a monument to this railway. Oare tunnel was used as an air-raid shelter during World War II, having its mouths bricked up, leaving only a small space at each end into which doors were fitted. After peace had been declared it became a cattle shed and remained such until recently when the tunnel mouths were unblocked and a rough roadway constructed along the original line of the railway to enable sands and gravels to be conveyed from a local pit to the main factory plant some distance away.

Nothing remains between Oare tunnel and Davington except for the concrete piles of the tiny bridge that crossed the stream which led into Oare Creek.

At Davington the site of the station and yard has disappeared under bricks and mortar as a new housing development, as mentioned earlier, has taken their place. The Faversham Society was keen to preserve the identity of this slice of history and hence 'Admiralty Close' came into being.

The engine shed has what could be termed a dignified retirement, standing erect in a hop garden at the village of Norton, three miles from Faversham. When the auction was held a Mr Brooker, the former publican at the Plough, Lewson Street, Norton bought it and used it for the storage of fruit baskets.

It is so easy for the railway historian to become a sentimentalist, but he must not overlook the fact that railways are constructed to serve. Bearing this in mind, and reflecting on the pages already turned, it can be truthfully stated that the Davington Light Railway did serve, but like so many of the faithful it now is amongst the fallen.

Davington station site in the 1960s looking towards the buffer stops.   *John Barnes*

Davington station site on 13th April, 1979. *Arthur Percival*

Admiralty Close in May 2014. This is the site of the east end of the Davington terminus. The trees beyond are in the grounds of Davington Priory. *Arthur Percival*

Chapter Five

Lost and Found in Brazil

When this writer had completed the final chapter of his book, way back in 1968, he thought that would be the end of the story. He had come to the wrong conclusion!

To begin with, news filtered through that a Ruston, Proctor factory engine had been rescued from a Cornish china clay pit and taken to Longfield, Kent for restoration. Then the writer heard that two of the Manning, Wardle saddle tanks had been discovered, without doubt, in Brazil. Finally, during the 1990s, additional information reached him concerning the internal combustion locomotive side of the operation.

On a lesser note, it was suggested by a correspondent that Gloucester Railway Carriage & Wagon Co. were the suppliers of the Davington Light Railway carriages, as this firm had constructed some similar toastrack rolling stock for the Woolwich Arsenal railway complex but to a differing gauge.

The steam locomotives

As already stated it is known that the three Manning, Wardles were returned to the makers in Leeds for repairs, and locomotive No. 1916 was packed for shipment overseas. The destination proved to be Imbituba, a port on the Brazilian coast some 400 miles north of the Uruguayan border, in the province of Santa Catarina. The engine was employed shunting coal wagons around the docks; and keeping it company was sister locomotive No. 1915 (Davington's No. 2).

By the early 1970s both engines were languishing in the docks in a derelict state, and it was rumoured that a third Manning, Wardle existed not far away at Capivari. However, the first-named locomotives remained in their parlous state for a further decade, but rescue was at hand.

The British railway press released the news, that the 'lost' Manning, Wardles had been found in Brazil, in January 1983 and the idea was put forward that some society or individual might consider bringing one of these locomotives back to Britain. It was thought that as few narrow gauge steam engines survive here which served on the military railways during the Great War, such action would fill this gap. Rival groups thought otherwise, they would prefer to see the locomotives preserved in their adopted country, Brazil.

This is the point in the story that the Estrada De Ferro Dona Teresa Cristina Railway enters the fray. Known originally as the Dona Cristina, this railway's seaward terminus was at Imbituba. Its purpose was to haul coal trains from inland mines to the port where the mineral was exported overseas. The workshops of the company are at nearby Tubarão.

British enthusiasts, no doubt influenced by the publicity given to the former Davington engines, approached the EFTDC with a view to its restoring the two

The chassis of No. 2 photographed in June 1985 at Tubarão works. *Chris Walker*

Inside Tubarão works the cab assembly, which had been modified some time earlier, and boiler undergo further restoration in June 1985 prior to the engine being put on display outside the works. The locomotive in the background is an EFDTC 2-10-4 built by Baldwin in 1940.

Chris Walker

LOST AND FOUND IN BRAZIL

One of the Manning, Wardle engines outside Tubarão workshops. Photographed in 1985, the locomotive was still there in December 1988. Note the absence of worksplates. This was No. 3, the plates were used on the newly restored engine No. 2. *Chris Walker*

The restored Manning, Wardle No. 2 exhibited outside Tubarão works in December 1988, bearing worksplate No. 1916. *Mike Cunningham*

Davington No. 2 preserved in Tubarão works, January, 2007. *Mark Smithers*

Davington No. 3 as preserved in January 2007. *Mark Smithers*

locomotives in Tubarão works and having them displayed as site exhibits. It was hoped that in the long term a museum could be set up at the workshops.

Obviously the request was received favourably for in 1984 the two Manning, Wardles were rescued. The ex-Davington engines, Nos. 2 (1915) and 3 (1916), were loaded at Imbituba on to the flat wagons and hauled by an EFTDC steam locomotive to the Tubarão works.

In June 1985 one of the Manning, Wardles (No. 3) was photographed outside the workshops and it was still there three years later, minus worksplates. Meanwhile work on the other locomotive (No. 2) was proceeding at pace, chassis, cab assembly and boiler were all receiving attention. When the work was completed the restored engine (No. 2), wearing EFTDC livery and bearing 1916 worksplates, was put on display outside Tubarão works. Further work has been carried out, as can be seen in the photographs taken on 16th January, 2007.

Appendix

'Who Killed Cock Robin?'

Whilst travelling to and from work the men enjoyed a sing-song, a favourite song being 'Who killed Cock Robin?'. There were others, but the employees of the Explosives Loading Company had a tune of their own the words to which were as follows:

> We are the ELCO boys,
> We know our manners
> We spend all our tanners,
> We are respected wherever we go
> When we are riding in a railway train
> Doors and windows open wide,
> We are the boys of the ELC
> Don't care a scrap about the CPC

The reference to the 'Doors and windows open wide' relates to the toastrack carriages, whilst 'CPC' stood for a rival factory on the Uplees Marshes known as the Cotton Powder Co.

Acknowledgements

This work has been very much a homespun product, and to mention all those who have kindly helped me with this project would be impossible, but to any who have been omitted I must now say my 'Thank you'.

Without the help of the Hunslet Engine Co. Ltd, of Leeds and to Mr Horsman in particular it is doubtful whether this book would ever have been written. Their supplying me with engine plans, maker's photograph and data was invaluable.

Among the local residents I must thank Mr W.E. Bunting, the late Mrs Mann, Mr Streatfield, Mr W. Epps, Mr Tucker, Mr Walton, Mr Busbridge, Mrs A. Epps, Mr W.E. Butler, Mr W.E. Davis, Mr S. Epps, Mr Lodder and Mr H.E. Grainge (now residing in Canada).

To Mrs L. Boyce and her colleagues of south-east London, I record my appreciation for their perseverance in the copying of old family photographs.

The help of the Public Record Office (now National Archives) is also acknowledged.

Finally I must especially single out Mr J. Barnes, who has painstakingly provided the recent photographs and diagrams for this book, together with his wife Joan, who has had the most laborious of tasks to perform that of typing and editing the manuscript, and my own wife, Veronica, who has forgone much in order that I might have the time to place this history before my readers.

Since publication Mr C.J. Walker and Mr M. Smithers have sent the author much material which has enabled the final chapter to be written. My sincere thanks go to Mr Walker for providing detail relating to his Brazilian visit together with photographs, and to Mr Smithers for additional information on the internal combustion locomotives and adding further to the Brazilian scene.

Thanks are due to Andrew Neale, who provided much of the new information on the locomotives at Davington and also to Roy Etherington and the Hunslet Engine Co. Archive, Maurice Dart and Robin Parkinson.

Mr R. Morris must be included as it was he who invited me to Longfield to see his Ruston, Proctor 'ZLH' locomotive.

This work must not be published without singling out Arthur Percival MBE, MA, D.Litt, FSA, FAHI, the Honorary Director of the Faversham Society for special mention as he has provided much information and numerous photographs to enhance this edition. Then there is Jane Kennedy, proprietor of the Oakwood Press, whose helpful guidance has seen this manuscript grow to a full blown publication. Thank you.

Bibliography

The Donna Thereza Christina Railway, P.E. Waters
'Preservation in Brazil', P.E. Waters, *Railway Magazine* Vol. 132 pp105-107
'Mystery Manning, Wardles in South America', P.E. Waters, *British Overseas Railway Journal* No. 1 pp 7-9
Railway Bylines Annual No. 1, M. Smithers, pp 67-77
Brazil - EFTC Railway, Ray Freeman Productions (Video)